Sorting

Peter Patilla

Heinemann Library
Chicago, Illinois

© 2000 Reed Educational & Professional Publishing
Published by Heinemann Library,
an imprint of Reed Educational & Professional Publishing,
Chicago, IL

Customer Service 1-888-454-2279
Visit our website at www.heinemannlibrary.com

Designed by AMR
Illustrations by Jessica Stockam (Beehive Illustration)
Originated by HBM Print Ltd, Singapore
Printed and bound by South China Printing Co., Hong Kong/China

04 03 02
10 9 8 7 6 5 4 3

Library of Congress Cataloging-in-Publication Data
Patilla, Peter.
    Sorting : (or handling data) / Peter Patilla.
        p. cm. – (Math links)
    Includes bibliographical references and index.
    Summary: Introduces the concepts of sets and subsets, exploring similarities and differences by grouping things together according to various attributes, such as color or shape.
    ISBN 1-57572-969-5
    1. Set theory Juvenile literature. [1. Set theory.] I. Title.
    II. Series: Patilla, Peter. Math links.
    QA248.P27 1999
    511.3'22—dc21   99-14552
                                                                    CIP

Acknowledgments
The Publishers would like to thank the following for permission to reproduce photographs:
Trevor Clifford, pp. 4, 5, 6, 8, 9, 10, 11, 12, 13, 15, 16, 17, 19, 20, 21, 23, 28; Oxford Scientific Films/ David B. Fleetham, p. 25 top; Tony Stone Images/Val Corbett, p. 25 bottom.

Cover photo: Trevor Clifford

Our thanks to David Kirkby for his comments in the preparation of this book.

Every effort has been made to contact copyright holders of any material reproduced in this book. Any omissions will be rectified in subsequent printings if notice is given to the Publisher.

Some words in this book are in bold, **like this.** You can find out what they mean by looking in the glossary. Look for the answers to the questions in the green boxes on page 32.

Contents

Matching Pairs

Sometimes things are in **pairs**. The pair may be exactly the same or almost the same. Some pairs have a left and a right.

Sometimes **matching** pairs need to be sorted.
It would be strange to wear socks that did
not match.

The socks in the picture need sorting. How many
matching pairs of socks are there?

Partners

We often **match** up items that go together.
Both pieces are needed to make something
work. A mouse works with a mousepad.

We match up things for many reasons.

We match up shapes, sizes, or colors of things.

Look at the picture. Sort the clothing into matching **pairs**.

Sorting by Use

When starting a **task**, we gather together everything we need. We do not want to forget something important.

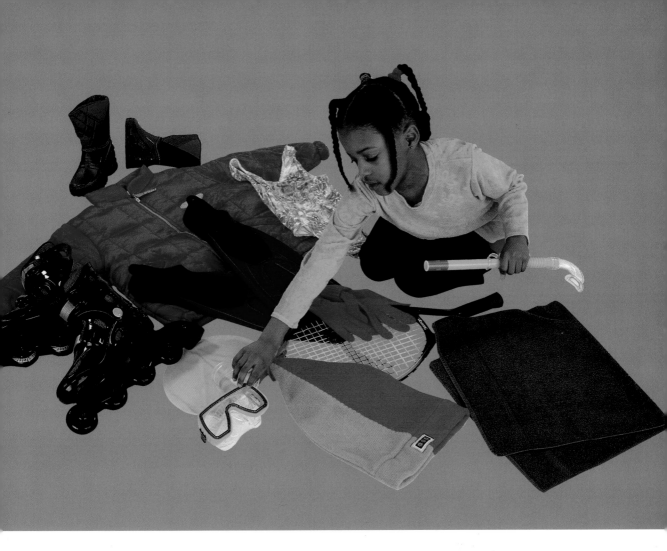

We use all kinds of things when we work or play.
But we do not need everything every time.

The girl in the picture is going swimming. She
sorts these things into two groups—the things
she needs and the things she does not need.

Odd One Out

Sometimes when we sort things, there is an odd one out. Something might be a slightly different size, shape, or color. Finding the odd one out can be important.

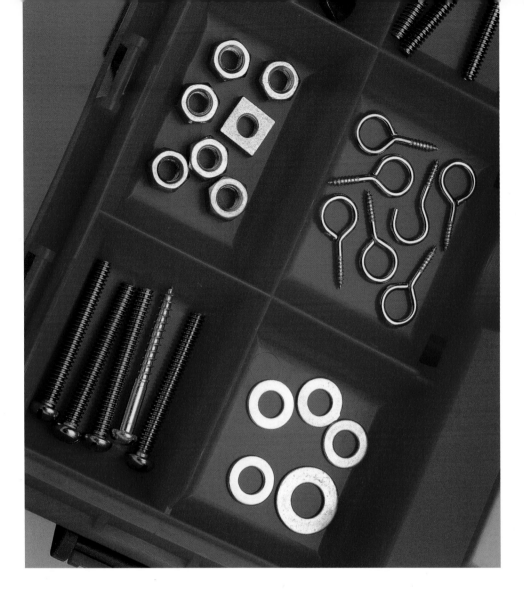

Sometimes things that are the same are grouped together. Then it is easy to find the odd one out.

Look at the things that are sorted in the picture. Can you find the ones that do not belong?

Color Sorting

We can sort by color. Colors are not always the same **shade**. We use words such as dark, bright, light, and deep to describe shades of color.

We can use shades of color to make a pattern.

Look at the picture. The squares are sorted by shade of color. What colors does this girl need to finish the pattern?

Shape Sorting

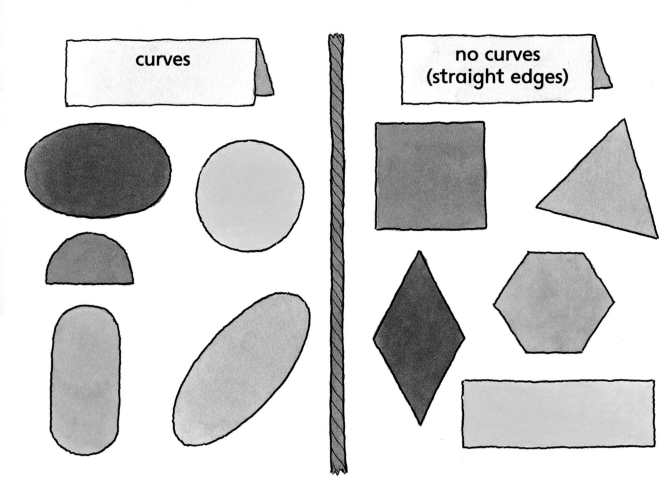

| curves | | no curves (straight edges) |

These shapes are sorted into two groups. One group is shapes with curves. The other group is shapes with no curves.

unsorted

straight-edged pieces

pieces without straight edges

These puzzle pieces are being sorted by shape.
They are being sorted to find pieces with straight
edges. Pieces with straight edges go into the box.
The other pieces are outside of the box.

Look at the unsorted pieces. How many more
pieces should go into the box?

Subsets

A set or group of things can be sorted into smaller sets. These are called **subsets.** This set of farm animals is sorted into four subsets. The subsets are ducks, cows, sheep, and horses.

16

Subsets help us **organize** things.

In the picture the boy is making subsets of knives, forks, and spoons. How many still need to be put into subsets?

Sorting Again

hooves

no hooves

four legs

does not have four legs

Sorting can often be done more than one way. A set can be sorted for many different reasons, such as color, shape, and size. These farm animals have been sorted two different ways.

Sometimes we sort the pieces in a game. Dominoes can be sorted into groups. One group might have dominoes with a **blank**. Another group might have dominoes with an **even number** of dots.

These dominoes can be sorted again. What other ways could they be sorted?

Sorting Two Ways

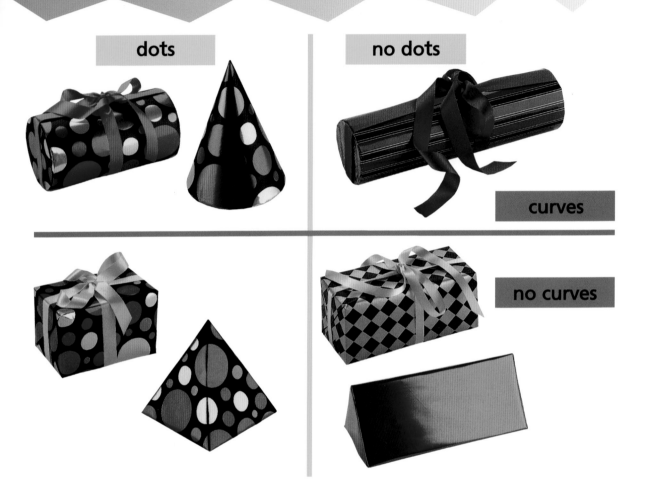

dots	no dots

curves

no curves

These presents are sorted two ways. They have dots or no dots. They have curves or no curves. Find the two presents that have both dots and curves.

This boy is sorting by color and by shape.

The color groups are yellow or not yellow. The shape groups are triangles or not triangles. How many pieces are both yellow and triangles?

Complete Sets

Some sets have to be complete. If something is missing, it will spoil the set. A puzzle with a missing piece spoils the picture.

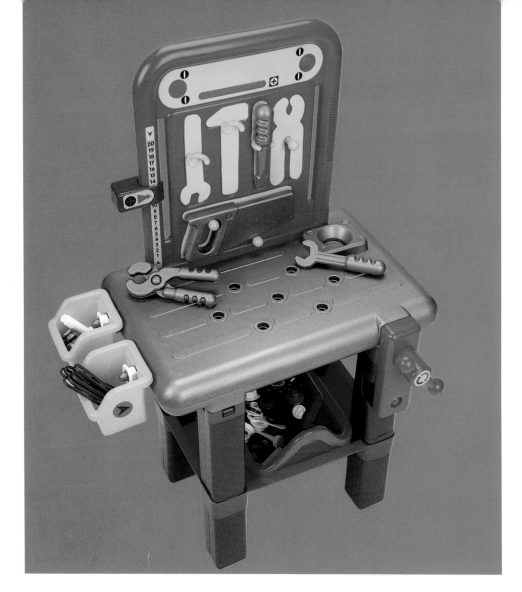

Outlines, **diagrams,** and pictures can help us
see when something is missing from a set.

Look at the the picture. What is missing
from the set?

Family Sets

Sometimes things in a set belong to a family. They may not look exactly the same, but they have a family likeness. This is a family of **rectangles**.

school of fish

flock of sheep

Some sets of animals have special names, such as a pack of wolves or a flock of birds.

What are some other names for family sets of animals?

Charts and Diagrams

Alex   Lucy   Mark   Anna   Maria

A **chart** can make finding information easier. This is a height chart. It shows who is tallest and who is shortest. It also shows which children are about the same height.

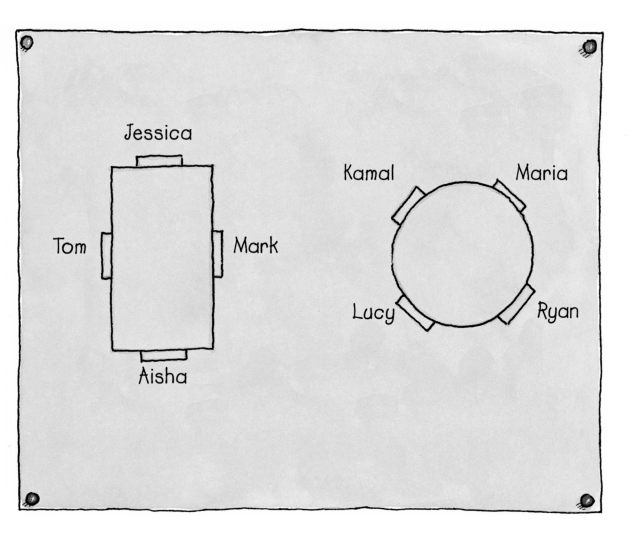

Charts and **diagrams** can be used to organize things. They can sort out where things go. They can show where people sit.

Look at the diagram. Who sits next to Maria?

Tables

Food	rolls	sandwiches	cookies	fruit	drinks
Aisha	I		I	I	I
Jessica		I		I	I
Kamal		I	I	I	I
Lucy	I			I	I
Maria	I		I		I
Mark		I	I	I	I
Ryan	I	I	I	I	I
Tom		I	I	I	I
Total	IIII	ℕ	ℕ I	ℕ II	ℕ III

This table shows what 8 children have in their lunch boxes.

A **table** has **rows** across and **columns** down. A table can help us keep track of the things we sort. Tally marks are little lines that show the number of things. The tally mark for 5 is five lines: ℕ.

Sunday	Monday	Tuesday	Wednesday	Thursday	Friday	Saturday
			1 swimming	2	3	4
5	6	7	8 swimming	9	10	11
12	13	14	15 swimming	16	17 Lucy's party	18
19	20	21	22 swimming	23	24	25
26 my birthday	27	28	29	30 go to dentist	31	

Tables can help us remember things. A calendar can be a table. The days go down in columns. The dates go across in rows.

Look at the calendar. When is Lucy's party? What activity happens on Wednesdays?

Glossary

blank empty. A domino blank has no dots.

chart place to write down information

column line of information that reads from top to bottom

diagram simple plan used to show something

even number numbers of things that can be put into groups of two with none left over; 2, 4, 6, 8, 10 are even numbers

matching things that are alike or go together

organize to put together

pair two of something, such as a pair of gloves

rectangle four-sided shape with opposite sides of the same length and four angles of the same size

row line of information that reads across

shade darkness or lightness of a color

subset set or group that is part of a larger set. A set of children has two subsets—boys and girls.

table way of showing information in columns and rows

task job or piece of work

More Books to Read

Cato, Sheila. *Counting and Numbers*. Minneapolis: Lerner Publishing Group, 1999.

Kirkby, David. *Sorting*. Crystal Lake, Ill.: Rigby Interactive Library, 1996.

Pluckrose, Henry. *Sorting*. Danbury, Conn.: Children's Press, 1995.

Answers

page 5   10 pairs

page 11   square nut, open hook, big washer, brass screw

page 13   one red square, one bright pink square

page 15   11 pieces

page 17   2 forks, 3 knives, 2 big spoons, 3 small spoons

page 19   odd number of spots, same number of spots, double numbers

page 21   2

page 23   the hammer

page 25   pride of lions, herd of elephants

page 27   Kamal and Ryan

page 29   Saturday the 17th, swimming

Index